CW00553688

EVELYN WILLIAMS *WORKS AND WORDS*

Evelyn Williams

EVELYN WILLIAMS

WORKS AND WORDS

EDITED BY DEREK BIRDSALL AND BRUCE BERNARD

OMNIFIC/LONDON

Title: EVELYN WILLIAMS WORKS AND WORDS

First published in Great Britain 1998 by

Omnific

9 Compton Avenue, Islington

London N1 2XD

SALES AND DISTRIBUTION

EYELINE PUBLICATIONS
12 Finsbury Park Road
London N4 2JZ
Tel: 020 7226 4916
art@evelynwilliams.com 720 3158

Text and images © copyright 1998 Evelyn Williams

Introduction © copyright 1998 John McEwen

Design © copyright 1998 Derek Birdsall RDI

Production supervised by Martin Lee

Work photographed by David Ridge

Typeset in Monotype Walbaum by Shirley Birdsall / Omnific

Film by Amilcare Pizzi S.p.A., Milan

Printed on Garda Matt 150 gsm in Italy by Amilcare Pizzi S.p.A., Milan

ISBN NUMBER: 0 953 2316 0 7

CONTENTS

EVELYN WILLIAMS by John McEwen

Evelyn Williams left the selection of the text and illustrations in this book to the expert eyes of her old art-school friend and subsequent champion, Bruce Bernard, and the designer Derek Birdsall. Like their acclaimed pictorial monographs of Van Gogh and Lucian Freud it is intended to be a work of art; celebrating the achievement of among the most poetic and humanly tender of contemporary artists who, on health grounds in middle-age, was forced to abandon her preferred method of sculptural relief for painting. The book documents this change. The text was not done to order but represents their selection from the spontaneous reflections the artist has written regularly since 1990. Each item complements rather than describes the work illustrated.

Evelyn Williams is Welsh and if her work is comparable with anyone's, it is surely the poetry of that earlier Welsh visionary, Henry Vaughan. When Vaughan writes of his 'Friends Departed' that 'They are all gone into the world of light!' or

Dear, Beauteous Death! the jewel of the Just,
Shining nowhere, but in the dark;
What mysteries do lie beyond thy dust,
Could man outlook that mark!

it brings to mind a Williams vision.

The definition of vision is an image conjured up vividly in the imagination. But a person described as 'visionary' means more than that. A visionary has an insight into the supernatural, even the divine. There is certainly a strong suggestion of the spiritual, the religious. Visionaries are seers, prophets, saints, mystics. They are few and far between, and rightly revered. Visionary artists are equally rare but the term has been vulgarised into jargon. Reading art reviews you would think they were two a penny. In fact in 50 years I have met only three, Victor Willing (1928-88), Cecil Collins (1908-89) and Evelyn Williams. It was in discussing Willing's work, someone she never met, that she once revealed her own artistic credo.

'He had the courage to expose his inner world, which is really what it's all about. When all is said and done, if artists have any function at all, that's what their job is. If in showing himself the artist helps to show other people to themselves, confirming for them half-known truths that have lain hidden in their memory, then that is marvellous; but if not, then tough.'

Meeting Evelyn Williams one is struck by her poise. She says she is not religious but she radiates the harmony associated with 'religious people'. She speaks gently but voices firm opinions. She has a ready humour. She dresses neatly in mute colours. She sits up straight. Her rooms are precise and shorn of clutter; colour is all in her carefully carefree London garden, with its bursting poppies and unruly honeysuckle. She describes herself as a puritan; surface calm, inner passion.

'I would like a canary,' she says, with regard to the decoration of her monochromatic studio, 'one spot of yellow; but to be so cruel would be self-indulgent; at least for the moment.' The wall above the mantelpiece is covered with cuttings: 'I snip them out of papers and magazines and leave them there till they turn yellow and fade away.' There is a series of people photographed first with their clothes on, then with them off – 'the difference is interesting' – another of close-ups of the molten effects of volcanoes. 'Volcanoes' is one of her meditations selected for the text of this book.

'I like to think of volcanoes from the safety of my room.

I am amazed at the idea of passion caged within the centre of the earth, spilling out explosions of fire when the pressure builds and showering the land with molten love.

In my mind I bask in the heat of the river of lava, embrace the disintegration of all matter to the boiling flames, and long in the solitary stability of my life that it too could be subject to such dramatic endings.'

She has harboured a dream for many years to paint a picture of nothing but flames; and she would like to paint a battle. In her work people wander, dream, sleep and bestow affection; but they also weep, plead, fight and are amusingly angry and lost for words. 'I don't like violence but I'm always anxious about something,' she says. And then there is her preoccupation with distance and distant connection, which may explain her love of sleep, that strange disconnected hinterland. The distance between a person's image of himself and the bare physical facts; between the individual and the crowd: 'I've always wanted to create the sense of a limitless crowd but it's always stopped by the edge'; the distance between the safety of her room and the unimaginable force of a volcanic eruption; between the atomic flash – 'a thought that haunted my post-war generation' – and nuclear devastation; between life and death. We met the week the space probe had landed on Mars, sending back its haunting images of desert infinity which looked like the backgrounds in some of her visions of loneliness. Mars was her latest preoccupation. 'It's so far away and yet suddenly it's in your sitting-room. I love this business of time. I like the idea of volcanoes and underground rivers, caves, tunnels and monsters of the deep singing to one another.'

So where was her vision forged?

There were childhood holidays in a cottage by the sea in Suffolk; but she concedes that the bleakness of wet, slate-black Wales, might have had even more to do with it. Welsh by birth though not by upbringing, she found herself evacuated there as a schoolgirl during the War and was impressed by what she saw. 'The apocalyptic landscape is the one I can relate to. The land is always heaving with the implication of some explosive eruption or threat from above, and uneasy – like the sea.'

There were also the peculiar circumstances of her schooling, which was undertaken at A.S. Neill's controversially experimental and non-religious Summerhill. Neill's ethos was apocalyptic and eruptive. He insisted children should be protected from their parents as soon as possible. It meant she boarded from the age of three, a painful separation she did not impose on her own two daughters. 'I hated it, particularly in the War when we seemed to be away for years at a time. My memory of childhood is one of sadness, a sense of loss, of being outside. Sadness has been with me for as long as I can remember.' Yet she remains an admirer of Neill, especially for treating children as people in their own right. Nor did it prevent her following in her parents' artistic footsteps.

Her father was a promising novelist, forced into journalism to make a living. He specialised in the brewing trade, 'writing features telling people in the subtlest way that they should go to pubs': but also wrote 15 unpublished novels. 'He was a lapsed Catholic and although he refused to see a priest when he was dying, I think he was always searching.' When he died she drew *Old Man's Dream*. Her mother too was unsatisfied in her own flamboyant way. She had once been an opera singer. Her death is commemorated by *Corridor*, the text exceptional in that it describes the painting; the excluded 'half-child' referred to being the artist herself.

IN THE CORRIDOR; A PAINTING

'The mother knows death is coming. She lies half suspended in the corridor, and death comes in a shaft of light.

There had been a second figure, a half-child. Pressed against the wall, watching. Her reactions were a mixture of dismay, a return to loneliness, and abhorrence. In effect, her presence made her a voyeur, creating an uncomfortable element in the picture.

Besides, her being there was unnecessary, for it is I who watch.'

What reproductions fail to convey is that almost half the works in this book are in sculptural relief. The reliefs came to an end in 1986 with *Falling Men*, *The Crowd Waiting* and *Portrait of an Anxious Man*. The decision was enforced by the need to protect a bad back, partially the result of making larger reliefs from the mid-1970s through the discovery of a hard-setting Italian modelling clay. The work simply became too heavy to handle and she gave it up regretfully. Williams still feels deprived. 'I consider myself a sculptor who paints,' she says; and once before mused that 'in another life I think I would have been happy as a medieval stonemason.'

It is a shock to find that one of her frilly flowers is in rock-hard clay and fills a wall; or that *The Valley* measures 143 x 226 cm. and its undulating segments of 'cloud' are topped with chunky spear-heads of 'rain' prominent enough to grip. The difference between these reliefs and her drawings or paintings is spectacular; the most obvious being that sculpture changes with the viewpoint. As she says: 'They are less static than paintings'. To stand alongside *The Valley* and see its turbulent grey contours adds a lunar loneliness to its meaning. But although they are reliefs they are also paintings; and even in two-dimensions she can give an illusion of relief by continuing the image round the sides. This teasing ambiguity was encapsulated when she entered two papier-maché heads for the painting section of the 1961 John Moores Exhibition and won First Prize for sculpture, causing a furore.

She did not start as a sculptor. Her art education, which began at St Martin's when she was only 14 and ended at the Royal College seven years later, was conventionally inclined to painting and drawing. She shone at both. As a draughtsman she won the RCA's prestigious E.Q. Henriques Drawing Prize. She graduated with a First Class diploma.

Her generation is that of the Kitchen Sink painters, whose domestic focus and unsentimental humanity she shares. Like her friend Jack Smith in his early work she uses a low-key tonal palette. 'You probably won't believe it when I tell you that before I start I spend hours deciding on the colour. You might well say, 'What colour?' But the little that there is means a lot – at least it means a lot to me – because it sets a mood. Swirling colour has always left me bewildered, and saturated colour can physically give me pain. There's a certain time in the spring when the yellow jasmine and pink cherry blossom come out simultaneously and you get one lot against the other – I get stabbing pains in the eyes if I look at them.'

There is certainly something Kitchen-Sinkish about the novelist *Fay Weldon's Bedroom*, both in subject and the robust drawing of the baby's basket; also discernible in her solidly shaded drapery in *The Watcher* and other instances where the twist or fold of a material is emphasised by shadow. But like all artists, to follow an influence is to unwind a ball of wool. She professes a regard for Spencer, it is hard not to see Blake behind much of what she does, but both merely open the doors to the deluge of the Renaissance, and beyond that the Gothic. Her work is full of Eves and Adams and expulsions from the Garden. When I mentioned Fuseli – and I might just as well have chosen his contemporary Barry – in the context of *Sea of Faces*, she said it was a drawing of a relief that had fallen from the wall and smashed, littering the carpet with apparently drowning faces.

The artist that may have had the most profound effect on her, her favourite as a child, is Gustave Dore. She still has her childhood copy of his illustrated 'Don Quixote'; although *Loneliness* is more reminiscent of one of his drawings for Dante's 'Inferno'. A favourite picture, revealed by chance in conversation, is Raeburn's *Rev Robert Walker Skating on Duddingston Loch* ('*The Skater*'), 'because it looks as if he's moving. If he'd done only this one painting that would have been enough'; and she admires late Goya, as *Rebirth* suggests. *Dream* has an obvious surrealist absurdity: and *Head of a Child* 1991 provoked a compliment for Rouault.

Giacommetti does not seem to have interested her as a student, though he was an art-school favourite of the time; but she did enjoy the 1996 retrospective at the Royal Academy, being particularly struck by the 'vulnerability' of his figures, a word supremely applicable to her own. Her cocooned sleepers have an unavoidable echo of Moore's *Shelter* drawings; but hers have a greater sense of human frailty and in recent paintings the sheet has seemed more like a wave than a sheath. Her sculptural work seems closer in form to that of Kenneth Armitage. Armitage's bronze *Forest* 1965, with its outstretched arms and spread fingers has its counterpart in *Imprisoned People*, though the mood is utterly different. The only modern artist who orchestrates figures in anything like the way she does is the German painter Edgar Ende (1901-1965), one of the few surprises in the exhibition 'Annees 30 en Europe' at the Musee d 'Art Moderne, Paris, in 1997; but she did not know of his work. In fact, film has probably informed her visual sense even more than painting or sculpture: documentary footage of Hitlerian rallies – 'I can never have enough of that sort of thing' – and, in general, the filmic aerial view. *In the Pit*, especially, feels like the view from some sci-fi space-ship, the camera zooming in and out as it traverses alien terrain.

After art school she briefly earned her living as a children's portrait painter, encouraged by the success of a commission undertaken for the architect Hugh Casson; but winning the sculpture prize at the John Moores Exhibition consolidated her desire to work in three-dimensions. For a decade she used wax for modelling, the colour mixed with the material, string dipped in molten wax for the hair. In her 1997 exhibition at the City Art Gallery, Manchester, of paintings done in the nineties, there were some like *Meeting 1*, which are reminiscent of these wax figures with the string hair. Size too had been sustained at the approximate level of the late reliefs.

Size is the other victim of reproductions. She has never been afraid of it. Her largest work is the painted relief *All the People*, which measures 252 x 252 cm. It is illustrated here in full, with *Sleepwalkers* isolated as a detail. Sometimes the teeming heads of her crowds resemble the tight-packed stamens of a flower, as even more conspicuously in *Waiting for the Day*. In *Two Sisters: White Flowers* the equation is stated. She wrote a text for the even more explicit *Sunflower* (not illustrated), where ragged petals hover on the verge of dancing figures. It was published in the catalogue for her exhibition 'Out of the Forest' at The Graves Art Gallery, Sheffield, in 1990:

FLOWERS

My late discovery of this new foreign population, not animal, nor human, plainly a species with its own definite life, was the beginning of a love affair. It was never a question of making studies of flowers or plants, rather finding a way of recreating their sense of aliveness, of their being alive.

My ambition would be to create in work a new species of my own – the final form being dictated by the growth itself.

The scale of her work can be as surprising as the forceful moulding of the reliefs. It is a shock to find that *Child Drawing* is a big picture. And her drawings can be even larger. In fact her second largest work in this selection is the 244 x 244 cm. charcoal on canvas *Whirlpool*. Just as her crowds can sometimes look like flowers, so *Whirlpool* suggests a 'ball' of fish, which is the protective way shoals drift in the oceans. There is an alternative text which reveals her awareness of the association (Graves Art Gallery, Sheffield, 1990):

THE WHIRLPOOL

The centre of the whirlpool both expels and sucks my people in. Like sardines, compressed and silvery and wedged together, their comfort the close proximity of their partners. They go through the motions of showing affection to the other, their grapplings become stylised gestures, cold comfort in their plight, while those whose arms stretch out in distress don't notice others whose movements have turned into casual wavings.

This metaphorical richness is what gives her work its poetic concentration and power to move, that and her openness of heart. 'In my early work I tended to show one person in a room and then as I developed I tried to relate one person to another and in time that got out of control and I finished up with hundreds of people. One does feel this tremendous pressure from the outside world now, of people – I mean, you just have to watch television.'

The latest pictures are for me among her finest. They delve deeper into the intimacy which runs like a thread through the 25 years of work illustrated in this volume; encouraged, as she admits, by the joys of grandparenthood, her grandchildren like 'Christmas presents'. It is expressed in several pictures of the most sublime tenderness of feeling, combining anxiety and awe: *New Baby*, the rough drawings for *Mother and Baby Sleeping*, the various paintings of *Mother and Child Resting*. Again one must resort to Vaughan:

'Happy those early days, when I
Shin'd in my Angel-infancy!'

Her extraordinary ability to convey the range of those aspects of human behaviour which lie beyond words, whether humorous, grief-stricken or in a truce of silence, has deepened with the wisdom of experience. Every parent will respond with a wry smile to *Child's Play*, where the adult is the plaything of the tyrannical infant; every couple will see themselves in the larger diptych *Togetherness*, where the battle of the sexes is over and the assailants drift back, not without some lingering acknowledgements, into their respective self-enclosures. And has there been a more heartfelt depiction of *Grieving*, that most volcanic of emotions? These are indeed 'bright shoots of everlastingness'.

John McEwen

The story of my life would go on a pin head.

I believed I could unfold my story as you would a carpet, with patterns emerging
and colours and shapes describing a section lived, each thread representing a different moment
and the carpet revealed would be seemingly never-ending.
Parts would be stained and threadbare, others singing with subtle colours, complicated themes and tranquil patches.

It would begin with the birth of a baby girl, pulled into the world with forceps,
a cowl encasing her head and tied about the neck.
The baby's eyes are tight shut for a week, while the mother lies in a nursing home too ill to bond with baby.
She is attached to the mother at regulated intervals, then removed by nurses until the next feed is due.
Those were the days when a baby's pram was put out in the snow to benefit from the fresh air,
never picked up between feeds for fear of spoiling, and trained to sleep at night by being left to cry.
This was nineteen hundred and twenty nine and this was how babies were nurtured.

The lessons were quickly learned: be good, don't cry, better not learn to talk,
smile and wonder with bewilderment why there was an absence of love in the house.
At the age of three baby is sent to boarding school.

One school, one childhood, unremarked but for recurrent images that would haunt her for the rest of her life.
A change of scene when war came from one landscape to another, but always the sense of loss.
The years were endured rather than enjoyed, for fun and childish pursuits did not seem relevant to baby.
A sense of responsibility grew as the child grew,
and a belief that it should be possible to alleviate the distress and pain of those around her,
in the hope they would acknowledge her own.

Baby has grown into a beautiful girl who is imprisoned in a glass box of self-consciousness,
unable to fend for herself but willy nilly thrust into the world at fifteen.

At twenty married to a boy she hoped would replace her mother, but found he needed a mother for himself.
Nevertheless, she had found a friend, and until he left her for another beautiful girl,
she loved him dearly, as he did her.

The sense of loss she always carried with her, alleviated to an extent on discovering she could create another world for
herself, made of line, shape, form and content.
Starting this process at the age of ten, she stubbornly drew and painted for the rest of her life,
always probing for a way to finalise the way she felt herself to be in relation to life.

When a baby girl was born to her she felt she was looking at herself.
Another baby girl later, another husband and friend, the family support that enabled her to function in the real world
and which provided the essential nourishment to sustain her.

Evelyn Williams

THE ARTISTS RACE OF LIFE

We thought it was a race for fun when we set off on the race of life.

The first runner holds the baton high and we all laugh as we begin, running strongly.
Now we remember the rules.
After an intensive burst, you hand the baton to the one who follows,
for you have played your small part, and must retire.
We didn't know then that once started there was only one end, or what retirement meant.
Here I am, at the head at last.
The race has become increasingly exhausting, and the baton I hold above represents my efforts
and all the efforts of my friends over a lifetime.
The shared activity was what united us, however different our interests.

I have now been running for a life time and feel the hot breath of a younger contestant on my neck.

Soon it will be time to hand over the symbol of struggle I hold so tightly and then to join my friends.

TOGETHERNESS

One day I turned around and found I was old.

The person I have always been, hidden, convinces me I am as I was.
The mirror tells me there is this other person, the impostor,
who lives for me, speaks for me,
carries me about and slowly suffocates me.

I would like to call a truce, a pact, for though not starting out together,
we are now fused irrevocably and surely must end together.

Much better to do this as friends than enemies.

CANDLE FLAMES

Waiting for the children reminds me that I live and breathe.
They burst on the world as characters in a play would, a play without beginnings or endings.
From them in turn will come more and each flame from candles mirrored in their eyes
multiply until they resemble stars blinking from a great distance.

As my light fades does theirs grow.
The flames are rising and falling, depending on our breath, depending on their laughter.

BLACK DOG

The days I keep the black dog at bay I notch up as a plus for me.

The days I feel his hot breath on my neck I endure in the knowledge he may not be there tomorrow.

But good days and bad days I know I was unable to take something out of life for myself,
that I couldn't grasp hold of what I wanted most.

I never knew what I wanted most.

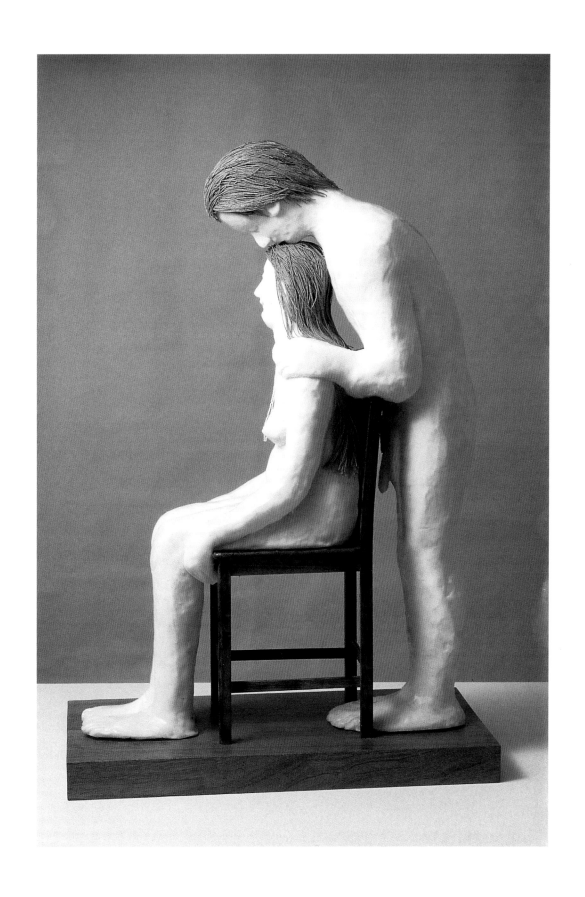

PROMISES

When young I made promises.

To love and to cherish, to be available by day and by night.
Ready to administer, to console, and to understand.
To be the steady rock against which others' waves washed, washing me away.

TENSION

As one line can't exist without another, so drawing is to do with tension.

Making constant adjustments, from one line to another, is what drawing is.
It's spilled over to how I see myself in relation to life.

When walking I am constantly judging the distance from myself to objects in space,
each step I take changes the equation.

There is invisible elastic stretching between me and the object,
a necklace made of emotions,
only when the tension has been tuned to near breaking point
is it right to stop winding out the line.

So with myself to people.

Friends and loved ones have an intricate web of lines between us
which (when things go right) give and stretch as our feelings for each other rise and fall.

When this doesn't happen the drawing becomes a scribble,
lines tangle and become slack despite the painful adjustments that have taken place.
If the drawing succeeds it will be taught with tension.
The piece will agitate in relation to the rectangle of the frame.

When the line sags we are left with something that isn't drawing,
rather an imitation, a fraud, a shadow of what could have been.

UNTITLED PLAY

I am the actress unable to find the role that suits her best.

Untrained for the parts I played, at each stage of my life I found myself unrehearsed,
forgetful of my lines and struck down with stage fright.

The role I played most often, that of the child, wasn't to develop from a slow beginning,
since I was incapable of exploring it fully, to then put aside as one I was too old to play.

The role of lover was over far too quickly, that of wife never ending,
whilst that of mother the one I enjoyed the most, got the most pleasure from and the most pain,
and that of grandmother an unexpected bonus of unbelievable delights.

And that of the Artist?

I didn't play this role from centre stage in a blaze of lights,
but from the wings where the shadows are.

I could never discover any structure to the role, or purpose or plan,
but despite this it was as the Artist I found to be the most rewarding.

I was never able to find out the name of the play.

LOVE LETTER TO BELLA

Bella, shining symbol of my love and happiness, I had a dream you came back to me.
Later I woke and remembered you were dead.

Loveliest, crazed forgetful cat, so white, I see your stay with me differently now.
You were the ghost of what I always wanted, the bleached negative of the love I needed,
catmother, my Bella.

SUNLIGHT

Sunlight is like love, it scorches you up.
I stay on the side of the street that lies in shadow watching the lovers,
wrapped around in my cloak of envy and desire.
It keeps me warm and I spend my days observing them.

The road between us, now swollen into a fast running river,
has no boatman to ferry me across to their side,
and I am stranded here among the shadows.

DEATH FROM FRIGHT

It won't be from drowning, since I was born with a cowl covering my face
nor from a chronic condition, as they go on forever however long you live.
I think it will be from fright.

When I go to work one day I'll find something has changed on the canvas.
No other hand will have touched it, yet the people will have moved,
jostling for position and pushing each other to get out of the frame.

I think they might well be hostile, wanting revenge for my treatment of them.

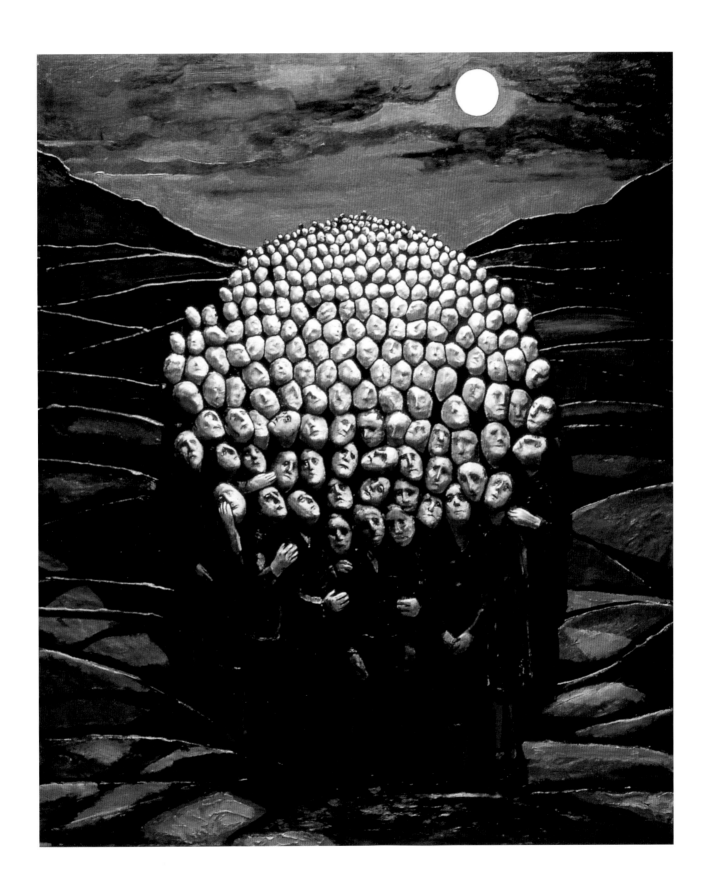

INSIDE THE ROOM

Take a room and the space within it. The walls are constructed from layers of our past.
The echoes of earlier occupants, ghosts of unhappy lives and laughter of previous generations,
faded wallpaper where the sun came in.

And the space between the walls?

That's where the secret hides.

There is nothing to see, but it contains enough energy to bring the walls tumbling down.

LIKE SNOW

It has been falling on me softly like snow for years,
and the taste of it in my mouth tells me what it is.
I can think of no defence against the despair I feel, nor an explanation,
and I don't see how to extricate myself.
I am in danger of being buried entirely.

FRIEND

Friend, if I can't tolerate my pain, how can I bear yours?

You sit in your shell in a room caged with sounds and images.
The flowers I gave you sit in the vase which you forgot to fill with water,
their flower-centres gasp like fishes mouths and they will be dead by evening.

There is nothing left to say after a lifetime, nothing left to do
unless I take your hand and we peer down into the hole together,
to get ourselves used to the idea that its there.

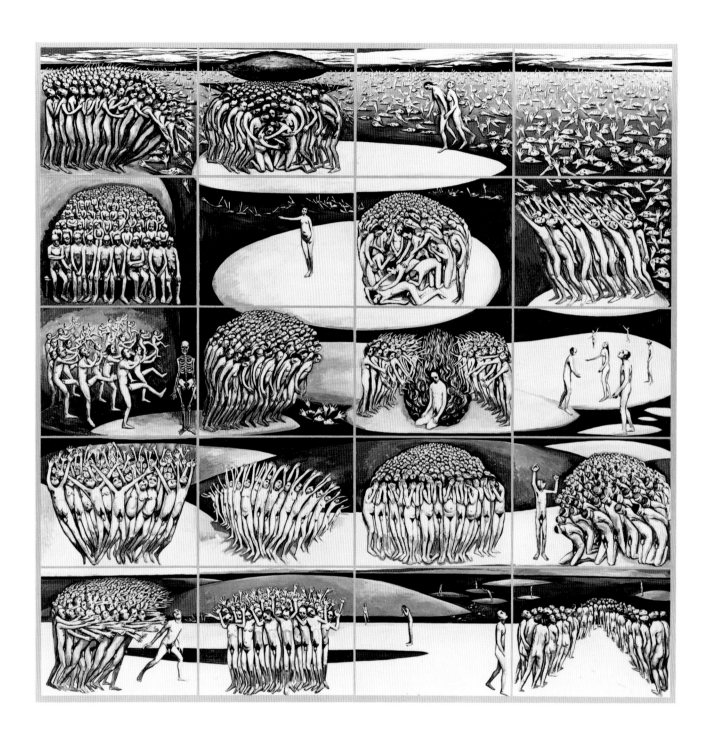

WAR

You see a child walking on tiptoe, an old man shouting to himself in the street,
a woman passing by, staring at something we cannot see.

They are tuned to something inside their heads, experiencing a life we will never know.

They present a shell of themselves to us, a facade that covers and hides what goes on inside.

They're protected as if in a castle prepared for war,
for from an early age the drawbridges were drawn up, the boiling oil prepared.

For this is war, and depending on the outcome depends the survival of the vulnerable,
the unprotected, against all the others.

STORM BLOWS

Is it anguish or anger that trees feel when the storm blows and builds up a vortex of lashing limbs?

If you stand below the trees you could be sucked up into those thrashing branches
and be crushed to the heart of the tree by cold hard arms.

The cries and moans come from the trees themselves as they call to each other,
and not from the wind. But better than just standing there, as they do on calm days.

SHADOWS

Shadows pull me in.

I'm drawn to the space they occupy and the light has to make do with what remains.

It's a turning to the dark, an impulse to explore those velvety tunnels,

and if I have to explain my behaviour I believe it just possible Goya is waiting for me around the next corner.

THE CENTRE

I had thought that objects, a flower, a portrait of someone who lived and breathed,
contained a truth wrapped around by its appearance.
Later I perceived that what I saw wasn't necessarily there at all.
There was a veil behind which there were more layers, more to discover,
perhaps something quite different, and behind that a kernel of timelessness, the essence of the subject.
It is only by stripping away all the layers that the centre can be discovered
and the outside doesn't describe that at all.

AT DAWN

Only joggers and suicides go to the sea at dawn.

Behind my sheet of rain-splashed glass I clearly see myself swimming, bravely striking out,
determined to cover a distance that will be unrecoverable
and only then turning to check my moonface pressed against the window,
mouthing goodbye.

THE BOX

I am a fly in a glass box that the world knocks on from time to time.
The noise of my beating wings deafens me —
from the outside I doubt if anything can be heard except a faint buzzing.

How did I get here? The door was certainly open long ago.
Later I thought someone would come along and rescue me,
that I could join the others, live in the outside world and have a good time.
I tested the glass sometimes.
It was always too tough to crack and I was never strong enough to break it.

TRAVELLING AT NIGHT

At night I don't see the speeding landscape, I am part of it.
The road rolls away in the dark, the sky not separate but pressed onto the land,
and I am cocooned in blackness as though I were in space.

While the journey lasts, I am suspended in time, the road running parallel to my life.

I know there is no destination, and all memory of my starting point is long forgotten.

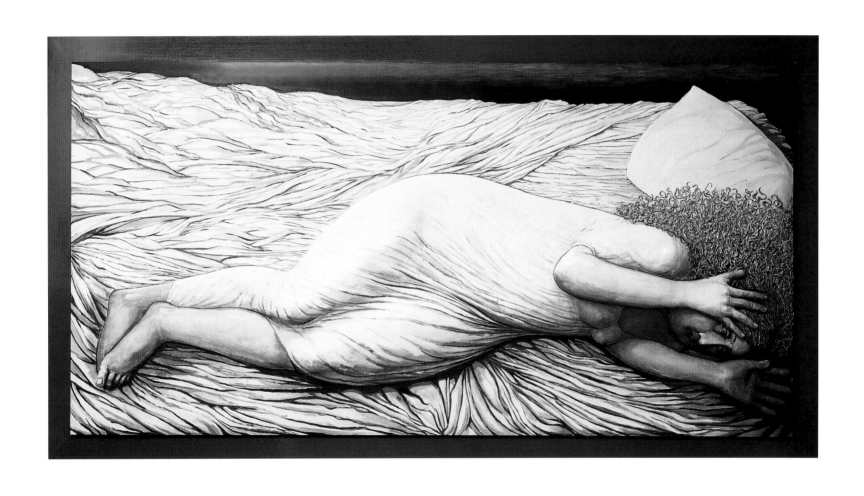

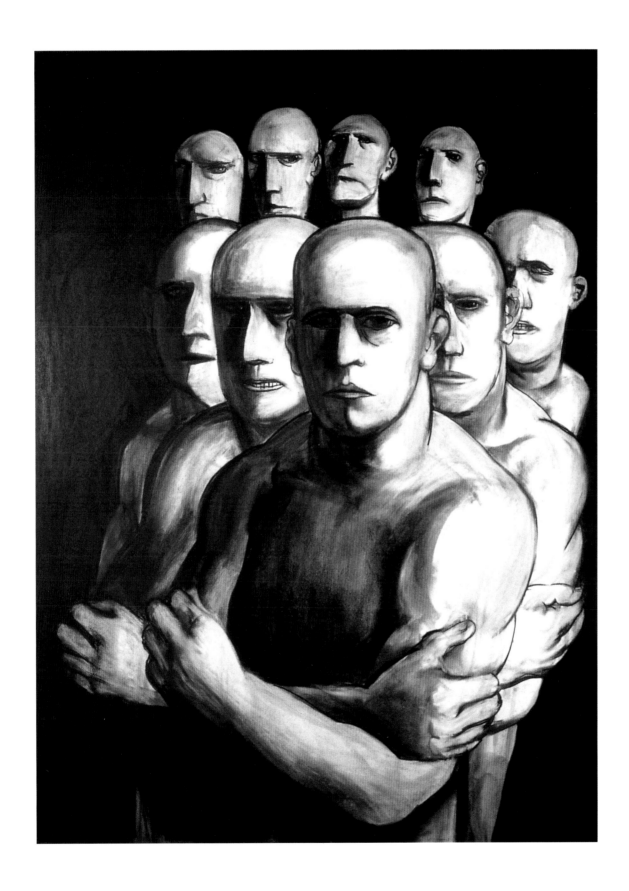

THE DARK

I thought I could explore it, and now it closes in on me like a hand at my throat.

I thought I had to be brave and, being drawn to danger, it has drawn me in.

I can see there is daylight outside,
but its as though it comes from some other world that flashes by as I sit in my sealed train.

GOYA

The smell of fear some pictures generate.

The background dark with something more than night,
more than black, an impenetrable wall of pigment that describes a state of mind,
a particularisation of a sense of foreboding and isolation.

A DROWNING MAN

A drowning man's life flashes in front of his eyes.

Here I'm going down for the umpteenth time.
This times its rock bottom, and I lie on my back on the sea bed looking through the layers of my life,
knowing if I could keep each one intact before putting it aside,
I would be able to find my way to the surface in time for one more lungfull of air,
and see the sky again.

THE TUNNELS

Each day the world turns away from the sun and drops into shadow as night falls.
Like Alice we tumble into blackness blinded by gigantic stars as we descend,
and our musings are our dreams.

The brilliance of light holds back the dark, illuminating the dome above us,
and the openings of tunnels which we dare to explore.

Now we have to hurry because the day is coming,
and the echoes of cockerels crowing are magnified unbearably down the endless shafts.
Each day we forget the excitement of the night before, as though it had never happened.

We live on the outside of the line and believe this is where the true world is.

WORDS

Words fall like leaves, each detached from the other and paper thin,
colour and meaning evaporating as they float downwards.

So a sentence is formed, one word before the other without plan or purpose,
the juxtaposition of each a gamble whether the idea behind the words will still remain,
after they fall.

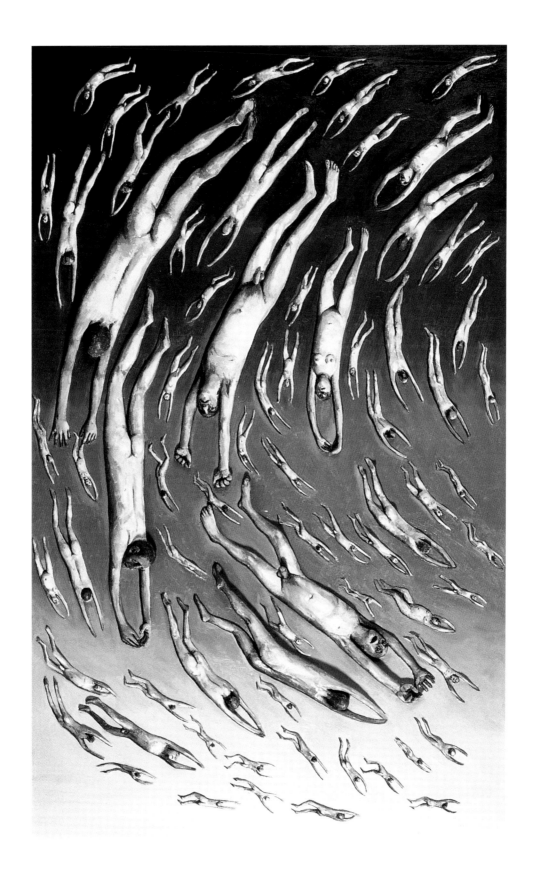

MY PEOPLE

"My people", who slowly made their appearance as groups and crowds,
silently congregating in ever increasing numbers, usually waiting,
sometimes making gestures of a kind.

Recently they have broken free and assume stances and postures to demonstrate their feelings.
Their bodies proclaim their intentions
like written banners that flicker and agitate across the paper.

Their message tells of their lives, how they feel, their inability to change,
their anger and their helplessness.
I fear this ever increasing army of people will lead me into a congested landscape
where I shall become one of their numbers, indistinguishable from them.

LOOKING INWARDS

I check my emotional temperature daily.

Where am I?

Who am I?

When I walk I look inwards.

I am absorbed in the sensations of my movement among stationary objects, my size in relation to them.

I feel like a flying bat taking soundings to tell me where I am
and I make sure to protect myself from the surrounding dusk.
My eyes are as good as shut, while my images come from glimpses, vibrations, memories of what I know to be true.

FEAR WAITS

Fear waits for me behind the door.
Some days he sleeps, beautiful wings curled over his face,
as I work to the melancholic song my imaginary yellow canary sings.

Other days he strides into the room like a boxer to the ring,
and there we wrestle until I accede him victory, for that day at least.

Sometimes blood is drawn, but mainly we fight with affection since we know each other well.

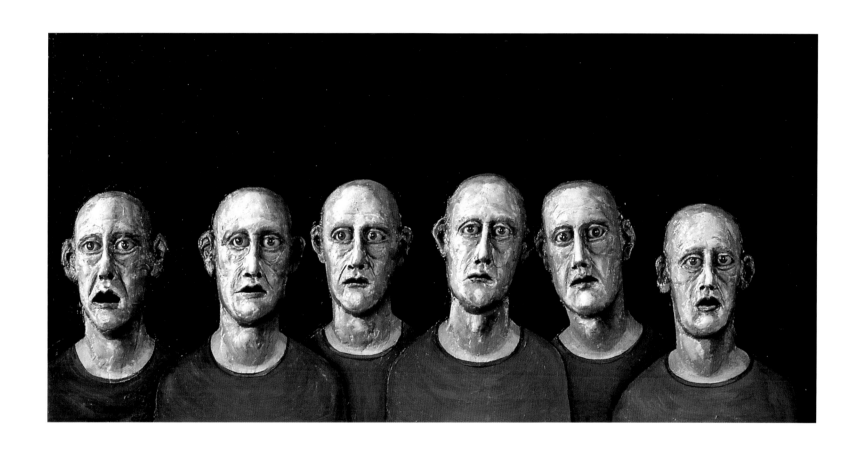

AGAIN AND AGAIN

Perhaps we fear death because non-existence sounds so negative,
and we've dreamed up the idea of an after life for this very reason.

We must try to explain negativeness in a more positive way,
see death as an expanding oblivion that is in a space which contains all the energies
we discharge at the moment of death, and take comfort.
Away with all conceptions of punishment, and thus guilt,
and regard space as filled with energy as the sky is filled with raindrops in a summer storm.
As each drop falls and touches the earth seeds of new energy are released
to be recycled again and again.

LAST LOVE LETTER

If I were to write one last love letter, it would be addressed to a compilation
of all the men I have loved, or admired from afar.
From memory I would select the parts I loved most about each,
and throw away those qualities I was unable to accept, or pretended to ignore.
My letter would be to a god-like creature such as the world has never seen,
and had I met such a person, my life would have been devoted to my loving him
and I would gladly have given all I had to give and more.
But these are dreams.

SHADOWS BETWEEN

The space between the figures holds more interest than the figures themselves.
The shadows that collect hold an unexplained mystery
and I find myself peering into them expectantly.
Should the last painting on the last day be all background?
And those activities and emotions that previously occupied areas in between
would be leeched away into a velvety space with a black hole in it.

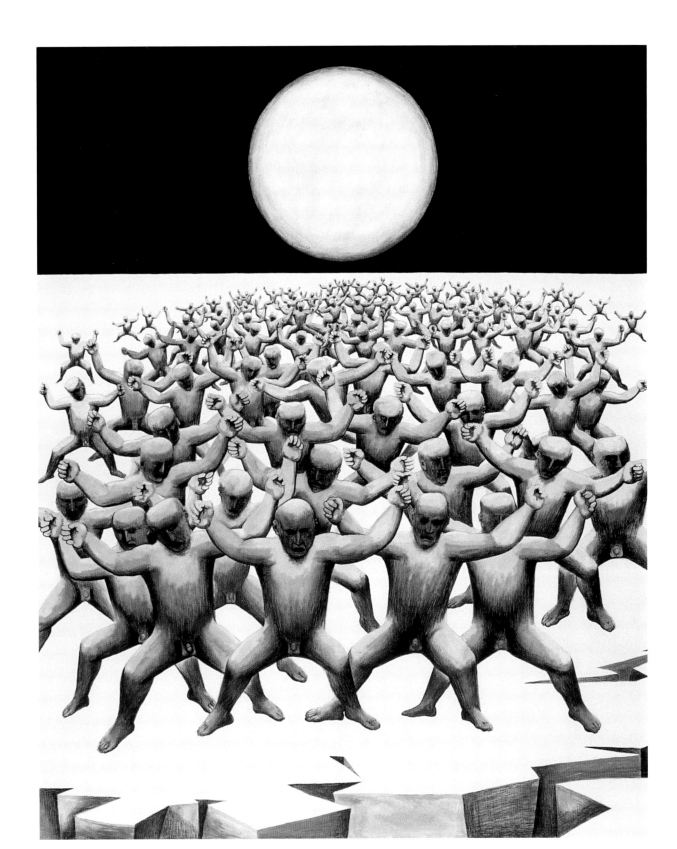

MY SHADOW

In the morning my shadow follows me, so much to see, so much to do.

In the evening my shadow precedes me – pulling me forward, here I go.

Where have I been, all the years of my life? Curious, aimless,
so much time and no life plan.

Through a silent childhood, then a woman.
All that beauty gone to waste, uncertain and apologetic.

Then a firming of resolution, convictions, responsibility and love at last.

Alas, feelings of restriction also, and a mirage of friendship with children that turns from a game of
"I'm bigger than you" into "I'm older than you".

Older becomes old and roles reverse. Now I'm the child, you the mother.

So tell me, when my shadow pulls me forward, shall I go?

AMBITIONS FOR A DRAWING

A drawn out sound, a variation of a note, like a whale's song travelling across oceans,
each note a tiny shift of tone from the next,
a build-up of restless echoes of a thousand other shapes.
More of a shimmer or quiver than a movement,
a ripple that builds as it travels across the surface, ending in pulsating forms that breathe.

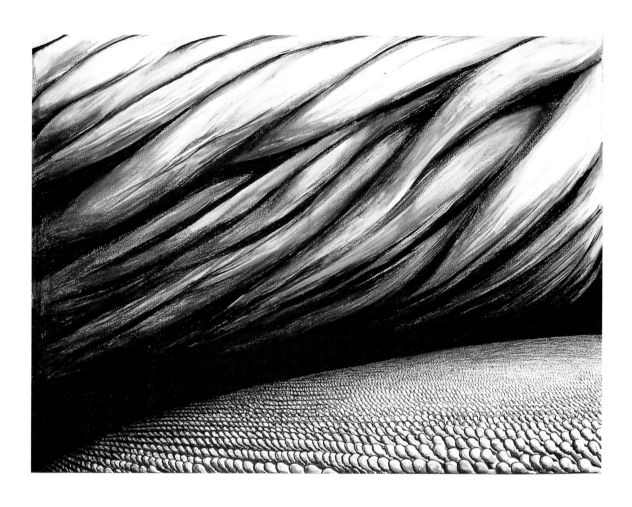

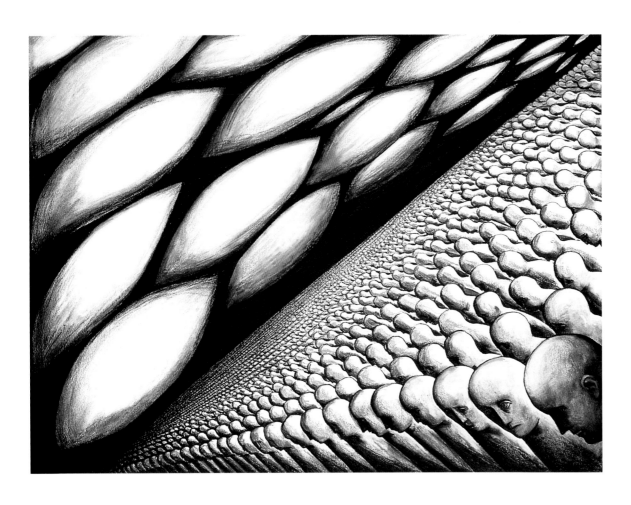

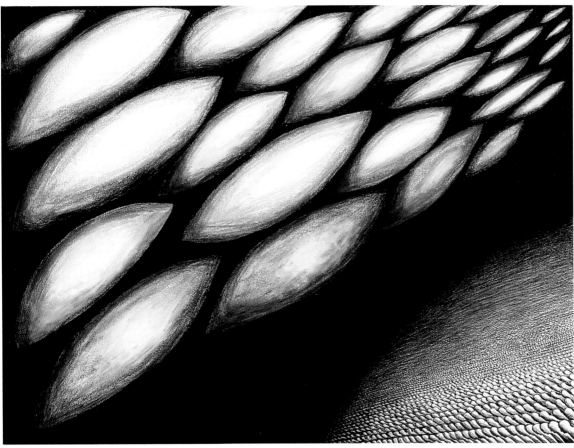

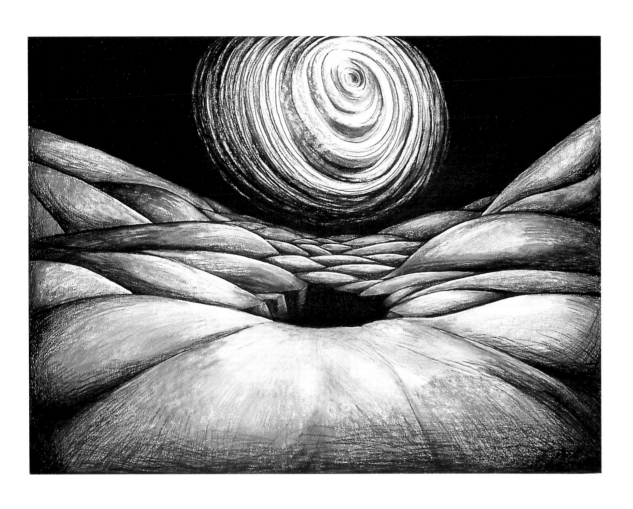

THE LINE AND THE CIRCLE

If all is circular and there are no straight lines in nature,
why do I keep bumping into sharp angles at every turn?

And even when the lines appear to curve,
we can't resist adjusting them to suit our compulsion for correctness,
and so straighten trees to conform to the idea of the upright.
Our love affair with the circle is rooted in our desire to return to the womb,
and our fascination with straight lines to avoid falling off the horizon.

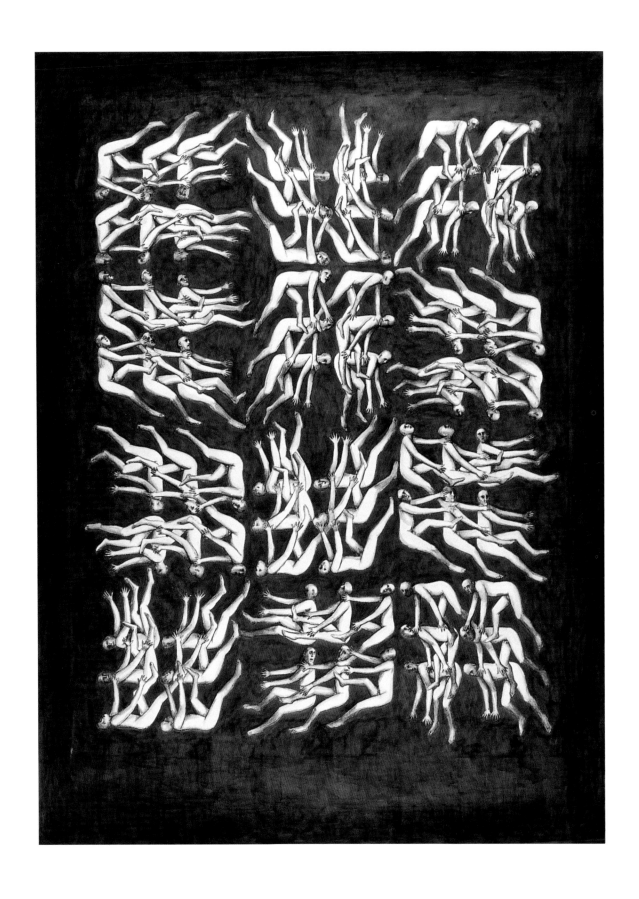

MEN VERSUS WOMEN

Men as a breed have ceased to interest me.
Unlike women, they are no longer able to meet their eyes in the mirror
and ask themselves who they are or why they are.

They have turned away from themselves in confusion and defeat
and now pursue power and status and wage war on each other,
while the poets from the past turn groaning in their graves.

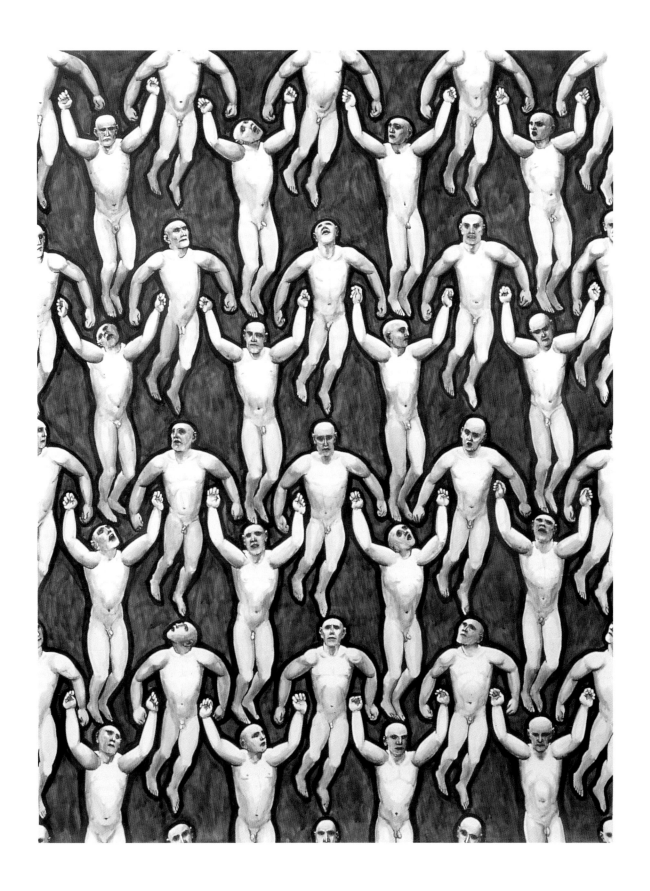

THE WIND CAVE AT LUCCA

I went to the centre of the earth and found a tiny blind creature there.
The wind tunnel brought in specks of food on which it lived.
It's pond was an inch large, transparent, deep in darkness,
above it a forest of stalagmites that formed a cathedral miles high.
There is no light or colour there, except the light I bring.

What does the creature think?

What does the centre of the earth look like when there's no light?

Is there a noise there, perhaps like the beating of a giant heart?

I put out my light so I can judge, but without light there is nothing,
and am I there?

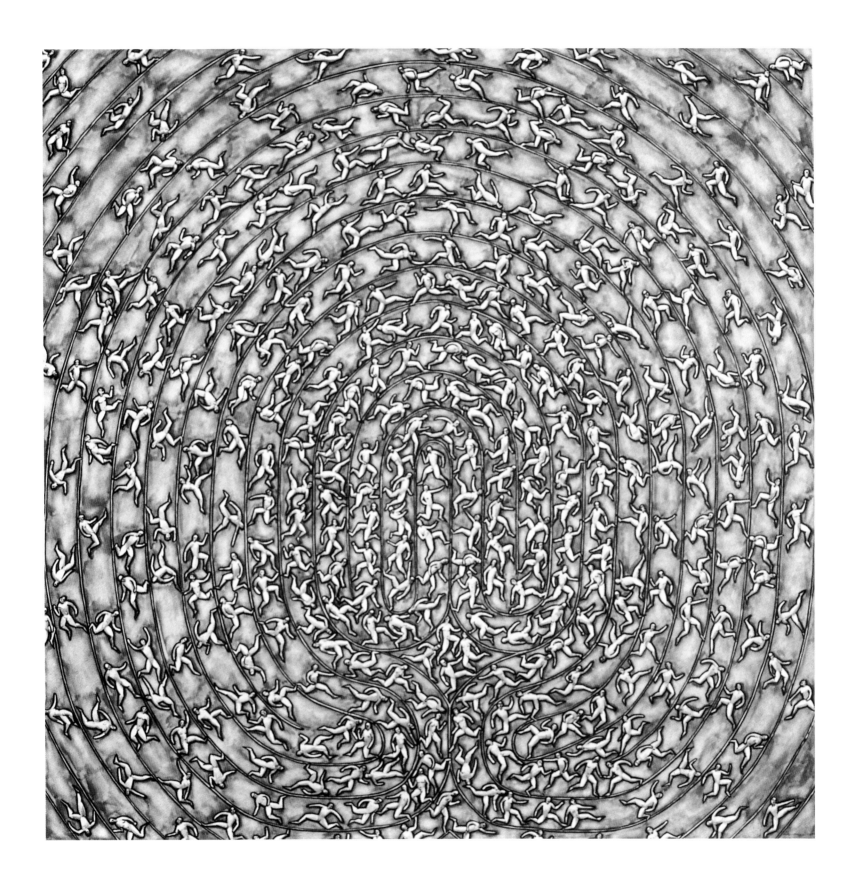

THE WISHES OF OTHERS

Each decision I make is determined by the wishes of others.
I have only ever seen myself in relation to those around me.
When asked what it is I want, I find I don't want anything,
but if I am asked to do something that relates to someone else, then this becomes meaningful to me.
When left to myself, I do what I do because I have already committed myself to it,
not because it gives me pleasure.

What gives me pleasure?
The rare occasion when I am outside myself and just being, free of the consciousness of myself.
The oblivion of dreamless sleep is pleasurable,
as is the experience of moving through water – the movements of the body brushing against water overrides all.

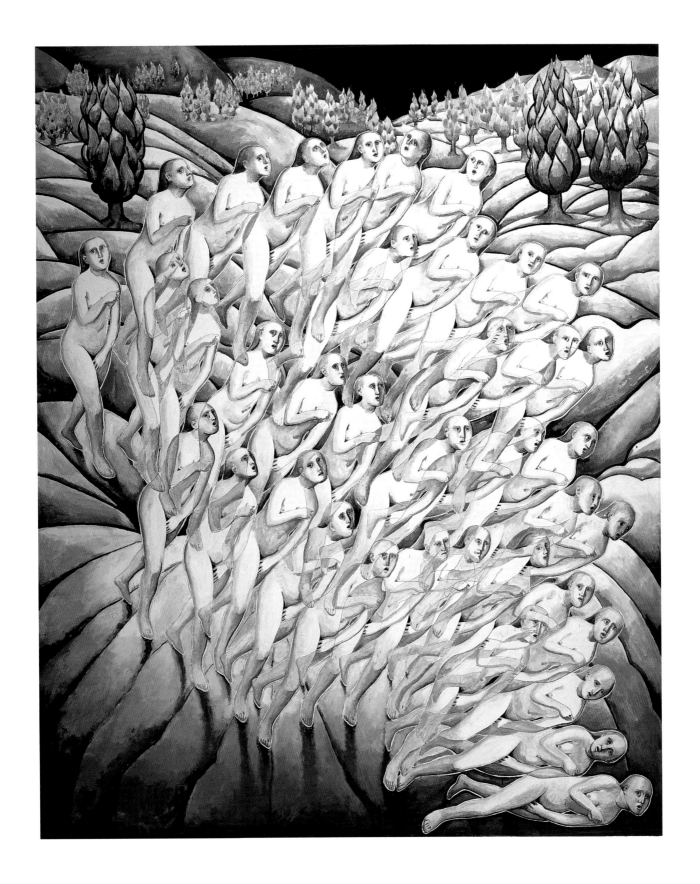

DETACHED

Floating free at last, with no sense of exhilaration,
more of alarm at being so brutally detached.
An awful desire to look back and plead with those I love not to let me go.

So now's the time.
I wrap my courage around me like swaddling clothes as I gather speed,
the wind in my hair.

DUSK

At dusk all space is vacuumed away, each object pressed against the next in an airless world.

Only our knowledge of a third dimension tells us that what we see are cut out trees and hills,
near enough to touch the far distance with our hands.
No light penetrates to illuminate the scene:
It is as though an invisible weight bears down from above,
and there is no wind to stir the trees.

We exist in no known element, strangers in a strange landscape,
and only our memory reminds us of the days that will follow.

STONES

I am given two small stones.
"So you can find peace".
The largest is filled with mysterious drifting smoke. I can't see into it however hard I try.
The second a tiny pebble, orange red like frozen blood.
I hold them tight in my hand and imagine them seeping through into my flesh.
Peace?
There is no peace for those driven.

A PORTRAIT

A portrait should shock.

In the tunnel of fear at the fairground,
an image will leap out of the darkness and scream at you,
to disappear into the blackness again.
So a portrait should jolt in the same way.
An immediate sense of presence that startles and impinges,
skinned of pretences, raw with demands.

Here is a personality, generously showing us the inherent emotions we collectively share.
If it doesn't have a life of its own the portrait has failed.

THE DIVIDING LINE

The line is a thread, so thin as to be unnoticeable.
This is the line that runs through everything, dividing the light from the dark,
you from me, the earth from outer space.

Its all but invisible, but like a crevasse that stretches forever.
Imperceivable to the naked eye, the shadow it casts is taller than the Great Wall of China.

Why do we find it so difficult to see?

It's because we've laid it in a minefield of other lives,
a spiders web enmeshing all matter together,
and now we've lost the ground plan.

A DREAM OF INSTABILITY

I'm travelling through streets where pavements steam and sulphur drifts.
I avoid looking down, hopscotching my way over the largest cracks,
imagining the scene beneath my feet, hearing the whispered conspiracies of my capture.
The buildings make me a giant, my shadow falls a mile away.
Too huge to be contained, I push against the houses.
Above, the sky is unstable with marauding clouds,
banging against one another like whales on the rampage.

MY HEART AND YOURS

The distance between my heart and yours is immeasurable,
 and the memory of our love is only a tiny part of the equation.

Standing on opposing mountain tops an ocean separates us,
among the waves fragments of our lives glisten,
torn scraps engraved by hard earned words and images.

Blurred and sodden by water, the record of our having been here,
all those unsung songs we wanted to sing to each other.

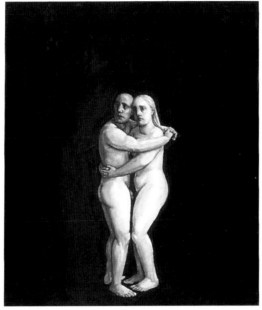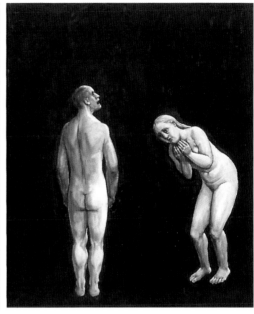

?

I see the world from the front; sideways, a sort of trembling, an uncertain wobble,
a doubt that what appears to be there is surely an underlining of a central misunderstanding.

Do I believe that what I see exists, or is it something that runs parallel with what I think I see?

I paint what I know and not what is here, and since I work from a memory that is unreliable,
how am I to know what is fact and at what point does memory stop and invention begin?

THE WOMAN WHO IS MYSELF

With scissors I cut up the photograph of my face in order to reassemble it.
I feel excitement and dread in equal measure and worry what the result will be.

Into quarters isn't enough.
I require dozens of pieces offering endless possibilities of creating a person with the same
colouring and features but resulting in quite a different being to the woman who is myself.

The work could take years to complete and already I sit buried in a silent rain of fragments.

When finished will the transformation go deeper than the surface of my face,
and in the process will my thoughts be scattered and reshaped into more interesting thoughts,
and will anyone recognise me?

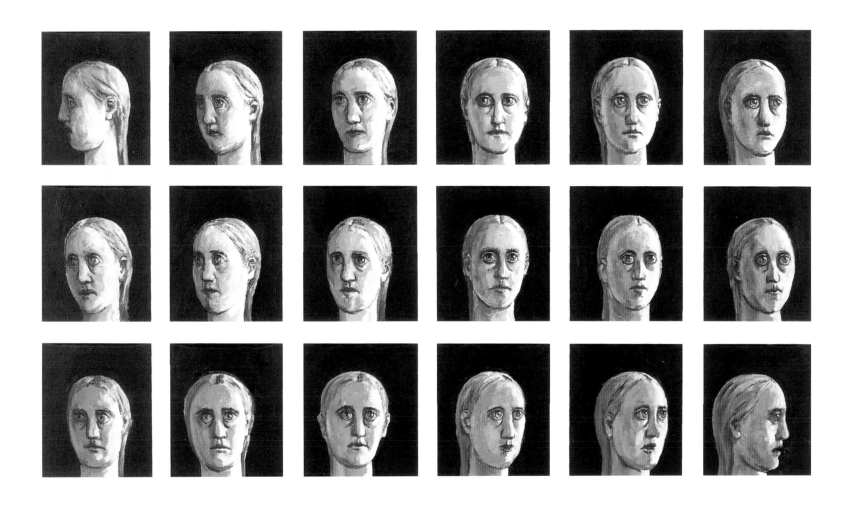

FACE AT THE WINDOW

The face at the window had come from my life
and she became images that grew into others.
Her face pressed against the glass became my history,
an ever present personal dilemma that ran parallel with my past.

Now I find myself living next door to such a woman.
She is partly a prisoner of her own imaginings,
but also a person stricken with an illness that precludes her ever leaving her room.
For years her moon face, chalk white, has looked out at the world.
What does she see, what does she think?

As I glance up at her window our eyes meet.
I ask her how she is and she says she's a little tired that day.
Perhaps tomorrow she'll feel better.

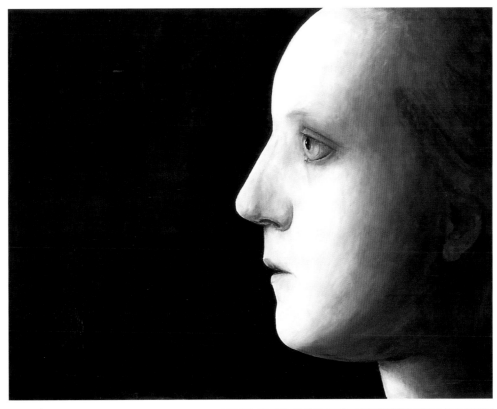

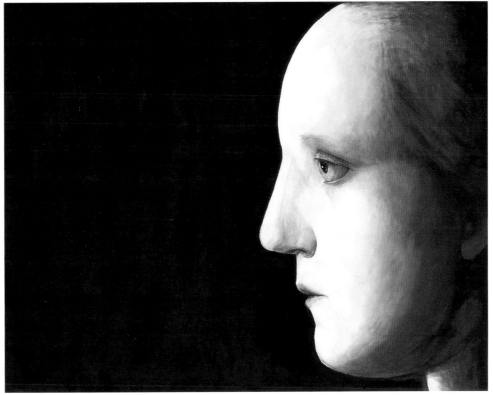

VOLCANOES

I like to think of volcanoes from the safety of my room.

I am amazed at the idea of passion caged within the centre of the earth,
spilling out explosions of fire when the pressure builds
and showering the land with molten love.

In my mind I bask in the heat of the river of lava,
embrace the disintegration of all matter to the boiling flames,
and long in the solitary stability of my life that it too could be subject to such dramatic endings.

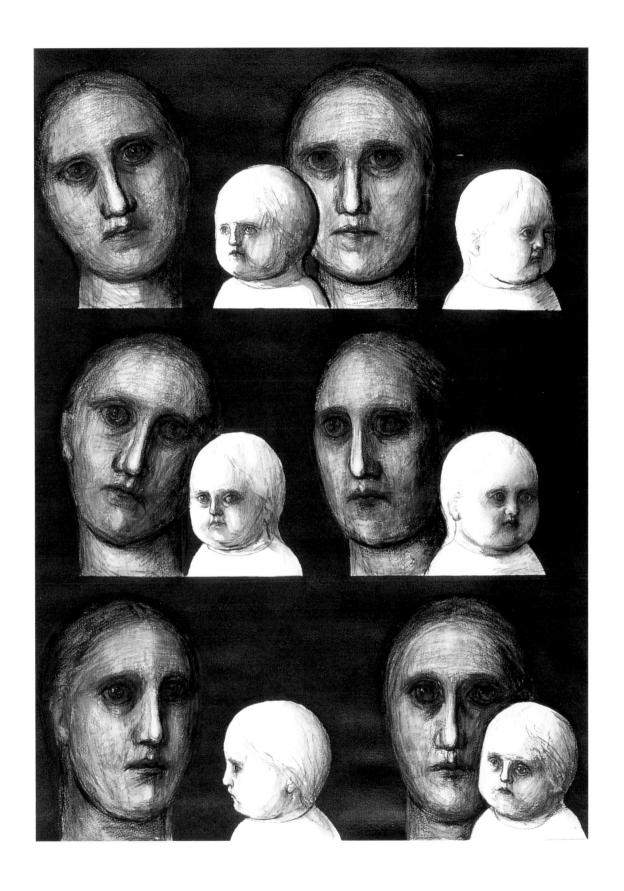

WORLD OF SLEEP

As my life becomes less eventful, so my dreams are filled with happenings.
Nightly I am transported into bizarre situations where I am among friends, strangers,
and surprised lovers.
I suffer dreadful nightmares and enjoy levels of serenity and sensations of happiness
unknown in waking hours.

Now I wait impatiently for the time to sleep,
hoping that this busy night life could be a foretaste of what's to come –
not oblivion, more a permanent state of extraordinary exaltation,
experiencing dramatic situations that in waking hours I have not the imagination to dream of.
A brand new life, to replace the old.

So the image of the sleeping woman is in my mind.

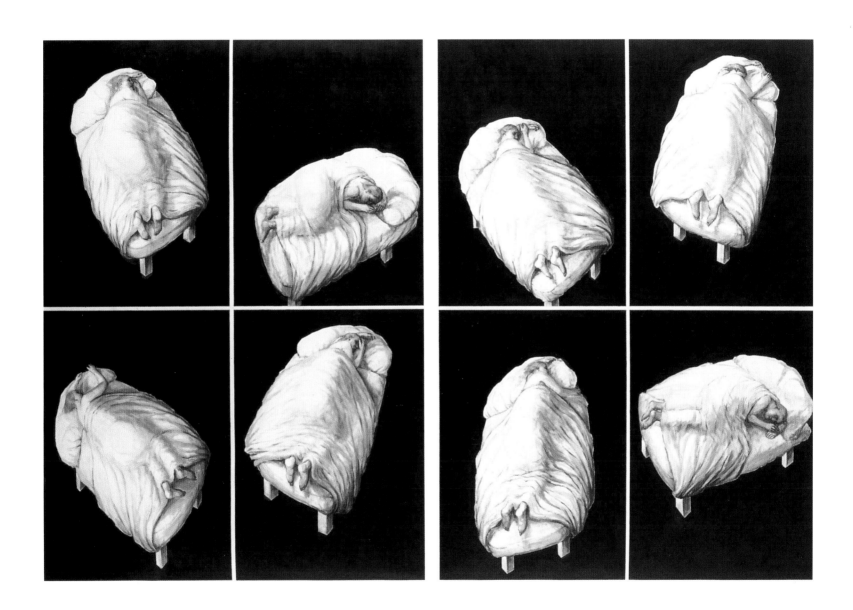

BIRTH

In giving birth the woman is momentarily part of the great universal plan of creation.

A seed full of magic has been planted in her belly
and in the short process of birth the world cracks open and a new life is announced
with cries, blood and gushing breaking dams of water.

The angry form is squeezed and torn, expelled with frightful force
from its warm dark tomb that has been the temporary cave of safety, its prison and only home.

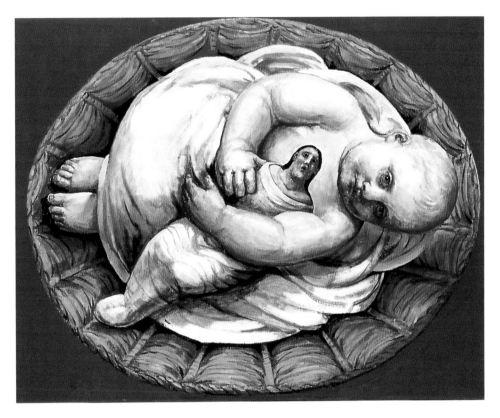

THE LINE BETWEEN

There is a line to be drawn between sleep and wakefulness
when I am suspended and floating between the two.
It's then that I listen to my other self and drift in this non-place which I recognise as a safe haven,
which I prefer to any other.

My life is illuminated by these states - they seem to have more relevance than waking experiences,
which cannot match the other for beauty and tranquillity, or offer such happiness.

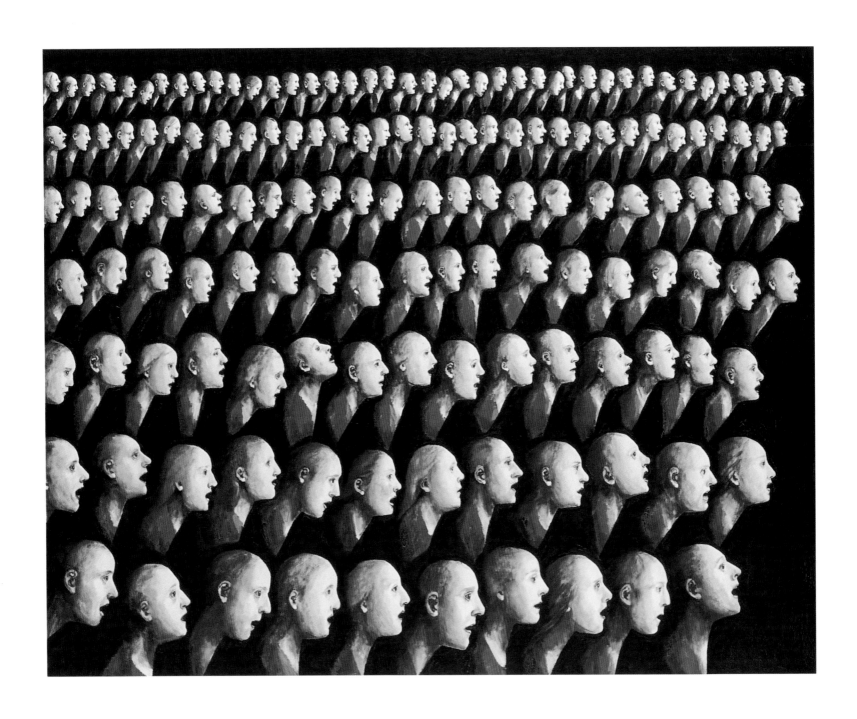

PERSISTENT IMAGES

The steadying influence of work protects against insanity.
Sucked into a world of illusion, a dangerous world for those with a precarious disposition,
I am in turn absorbed and infuriated,
seduced and repelled by recurrent images that chase me through my life.

My childhood was a vacuum, where pictures began to take shape
in an unformed head crowned with white blond hair.
I doubt if thoughts as such passed through my head,
rather sensations of pleasure and fear, isolation and anxiety,
and vibrations of others' feelings picked up with antennae grown in sympathy for the human condition.

But what form can you find to describe a sense of loss?
How do you find a shape to describe terror, apprehension and anguish?
And how to capture calm, movement of crowds, hands wrung in desperation?
How do you paint tears that really fall?

All these elements rattle around a young child's head like coloured marbles
and years later the ideas solidify and mature under constant testing, and once defined
are not content to disappear but continue to demand recognition through their persistence.

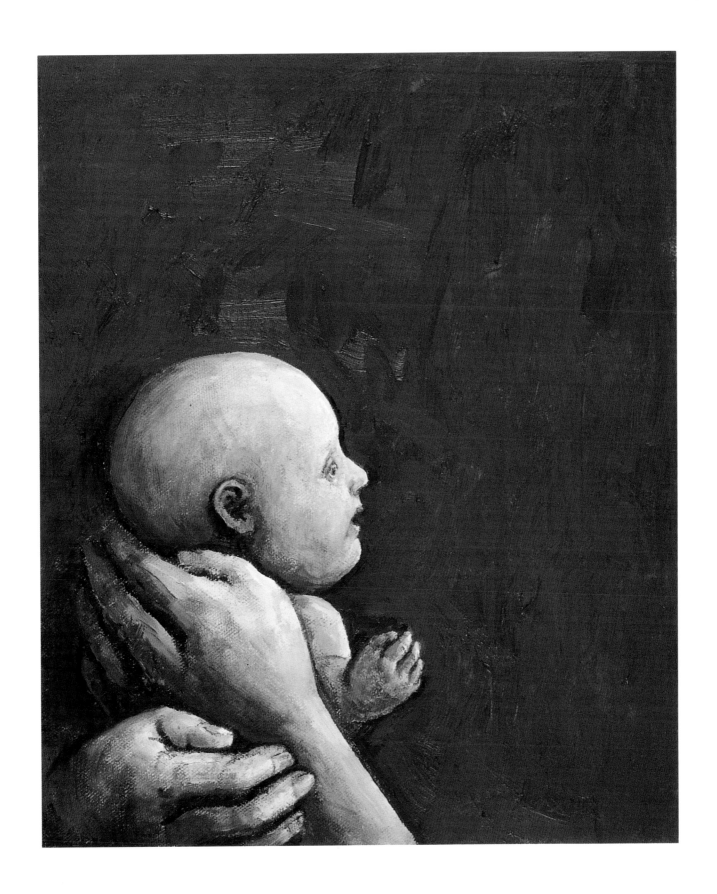

IN THE CORRIDOR. A PAINTING

The mother knows death is coming. She lies half suspended in the corridor,
and death comes in a shaft of light.

There had been a second figure, a half-child. Pressed against the wall, watching.
Her reactions were a mixture of dismay, a return to loneliness, and abhorrence.
In effect, her presence made her a voyeur, creating an uncomfortable element in the picture.

Besides, her being there was unnecessary, for it is I who watch.

THE DISEASE

Is there a disease that manifests itself in a person taking upon themselves the suffering of others?

What is its name? I believe I have this disease. In my case it's at the very centre of my work.

I take on the emotional lives of those people I invent, their thoughts and feelings and complicated relationships,
going from one image to another, one group to another,
hoping by getting under their skin and becoming part of them I shall be able to release them from their suffering.

INSIDE AND OUTSIDE

I approach the image from the outside where the surface of personality resides.
In reality, I am crouching somewhere inside the figure, imagining what it feels like to be it,
and searching for the outline that describes the shell of this particular person.
The outline is the furthest point from the core of this being, is fixed when the character defines itself,
and I am then secure in my knowledge of this individual being.

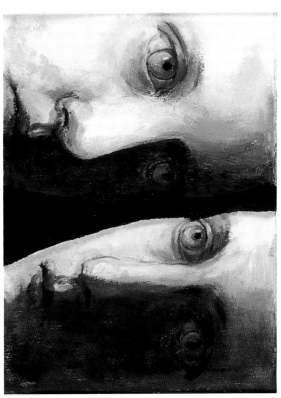

ABOUT DROWNING

How badly I was served by my teachers.
They taught the coward's way of painting.

The suggestion was that (with care) a painting would get better and better and when best,
be finished.

No talk of the image that was paramount, or that the task was to set the image free,
the probable result being not better, possibly worse,
but becoming in effect itself, an idea that lived and breathed.
This process can be a terrifying one, an unknown sea,
and painting more about drowning than swimming for the shore.

Certainly there are no cheering crowds with banners waiting by the edge of the sea,
but dark cliffs casting shadows over the water.

QUESTIONS

Is this what I see?

Is what I see there?

Is that all there is?

STATE OF REVERIE

My state of reverie is maintained by close attention to the physical details of my life.

Protected from and on occasion engulfed by the trivia of existence,
my goal has always been to find the moment when all goes still,
when my heart cucooned in calm allows the tiny seed of an idea to grow.
From such tenuous beginnings the embryo of an image will form.

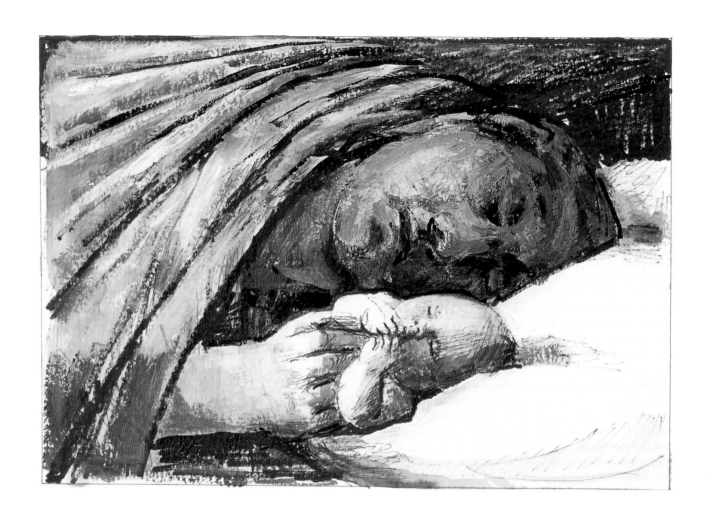

WORDS

To use words as a method of description holds no interest for me.

Seemingly sentences have to have a beginning, a middle and an end,
a build up of agreed words that describe a scene like a carpet slowly unravelled before your eyes.

Narrative carries you along to an arranged goal, while structure supports the tower of words.
The time it takes to read a paragraph becomes an element that is part of the whole,
while each word is dependent on the next, determined by its neighbour and irrelevant on its own.

Unlike writing, when descriptive realism is used in painting it is possible to describe an outer surface or shell
while simultaneously suggesting other dimensions of inner thoughts, other worlds.
On first sight you grasp the idea immediately from the centre,
later to explore the whole in all the depths and complexities of the piece.

What is of interest is to use words as a parallel dimension,
that add thoughts and ideas no colour or shape can describe.

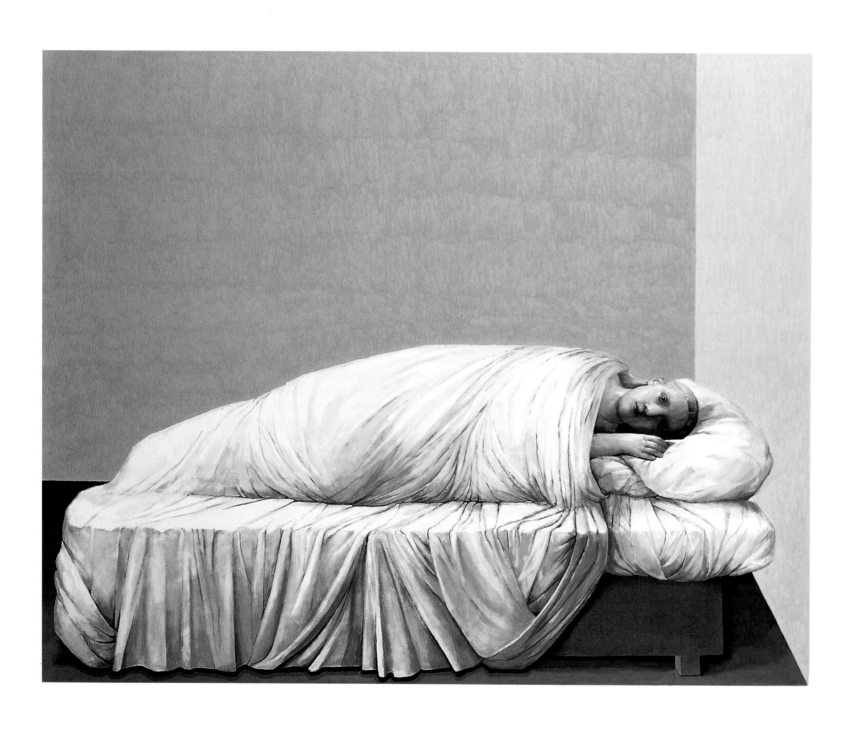

TIGHTROPE

In another life I would have walked the tightrope.
Dressed in spangles glittering in a searchlight,
with a bird's eye view of heads turned up to me,
I should parade my skills with bravado and prettiness,
wearing fishnet tights and emerald eyelashes and tiny scarlet slippers.

But I have this recurrent dream:
In my dream I walk the tightrope, high up at night through the dark of a distant landscape.
I have no net beneath me, the cold wind threatens with its gusts,
and my only company telegraph poles. Far below a house, my house, the windows lit.
The tightrope goes on as far as I can see, there is no way of getting off,
and the rope has grown slippery.
Is the distance between me and the ground now greater, or have I become taller?

TWO LIVES

I have always lived two lives.
Briefly, in the middle somewhere, there was a fusion of one to the other,
and I felt a sense of wholeness and unity.

As time went on, the balance was way over to the other side,
and now my anchorage has slipped,
and my first life is so far in the distant past I can just see it disappearing over the horizon.

FRESH AIR

Into the sour space vacuumed of all oxygen, a great burst of fresh air came and with it you,
so smooth, creamy and alert, giving off sparkles of beauty remembered from long ago.
Your name is youth and I recognise you from when I also felt myself to be faultless,
a perfect covering of new skin on a perfect frame.

DREAM NO. 1

In the dream I know that the time has come and I am climbing a steep incline in a wild landscape.

I am prepared to die and travel over the rough ground calmly but with difficulty
because of the stones and uneven surface.

I know that when I find the right place all I have to do is lie very still and wait.
When I select the spot I recognise the landscape as one of my own — each stick and stone
and blade of grass has been drawn by me in charcoal and chalks on to a flat surface,
the short strokes and lines of the drawing are rubbing off on me and I am becoming part of my imagined landscape.

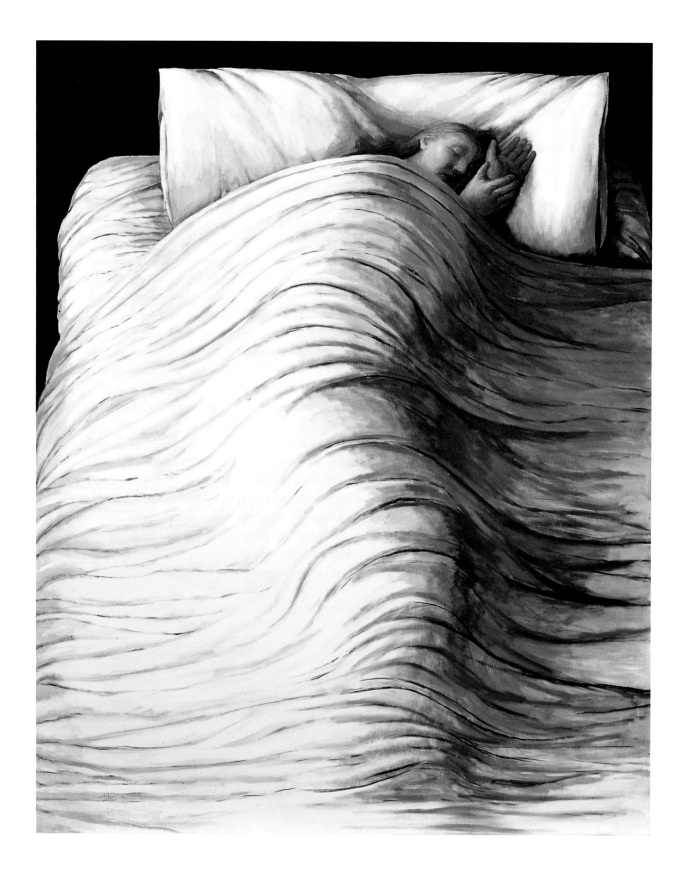

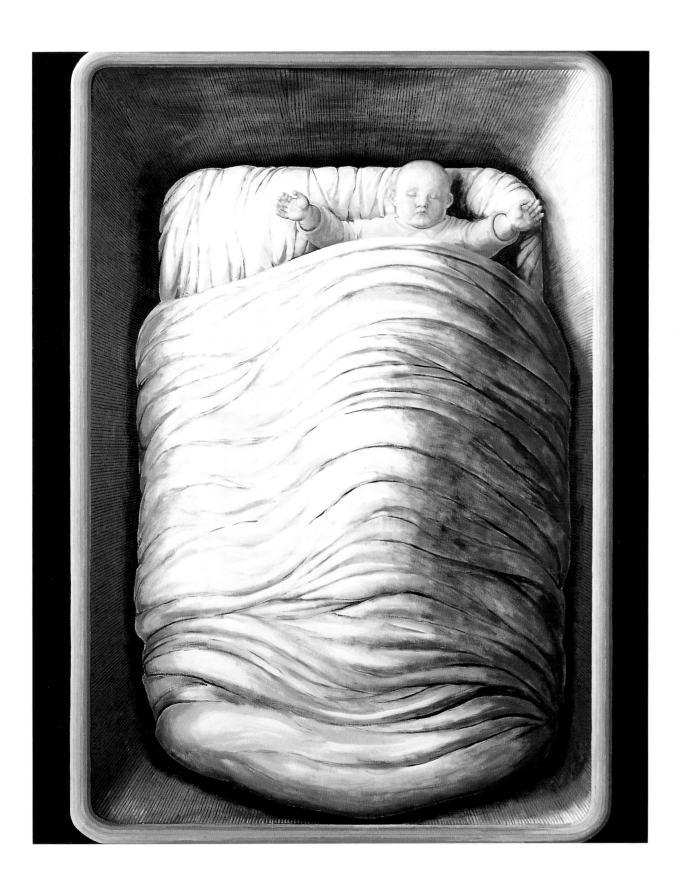

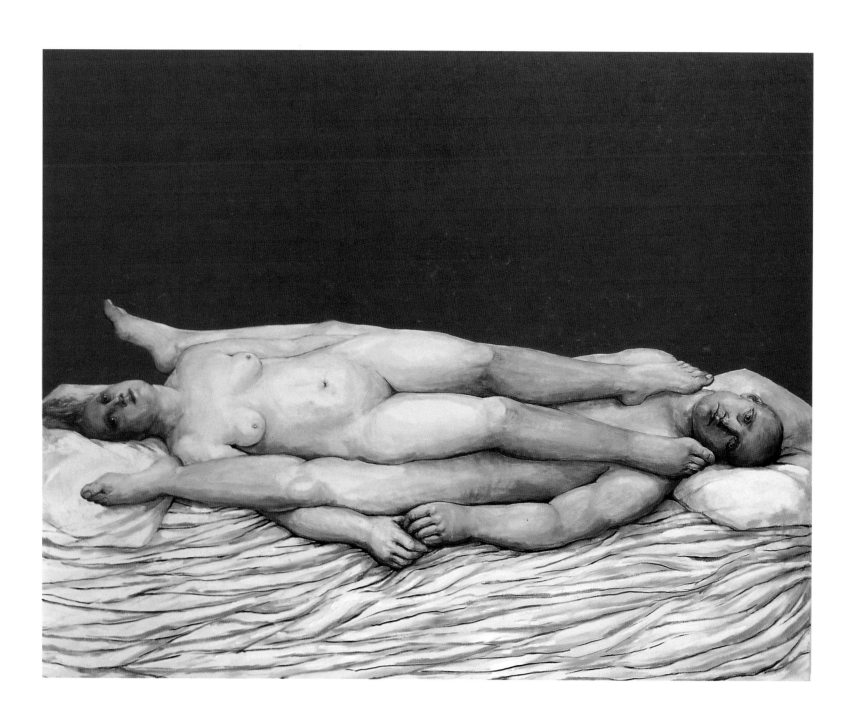

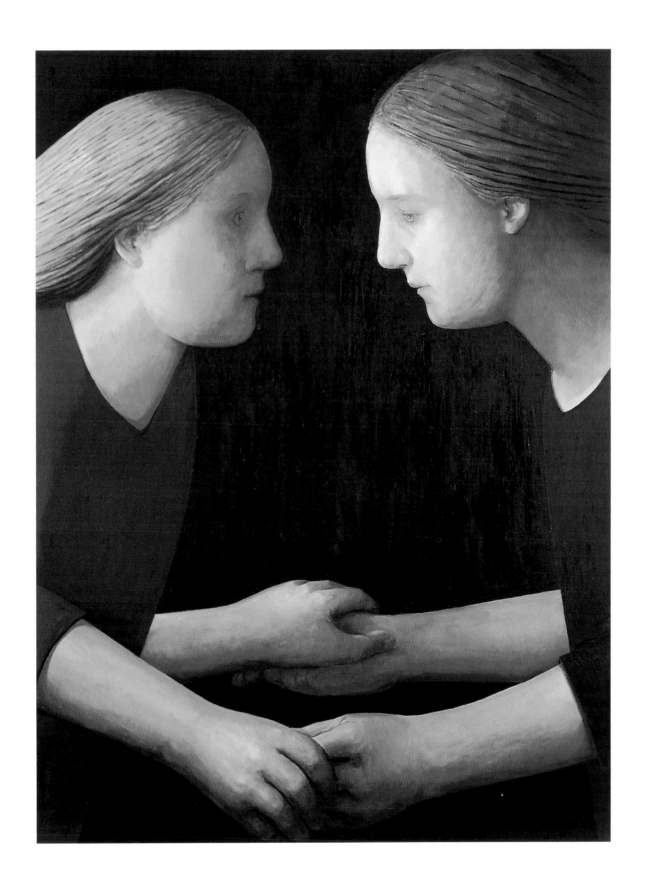

A HEAD TURNING

A head turning from the light describes a thinking process,
the mood changing from light to dark and in turning explains the passing of time,
it introduces animation and a sense of life.

It suggests a beginning, a middle and an end.
The passage between birth and death, a source outside ourselves,
illumination and shadow which rests on the surface, changing our appearance
but not the fundamental form we have manufactured for ourselves.

It confirms that should the source of light be interrupted or disappear, something will still remain.

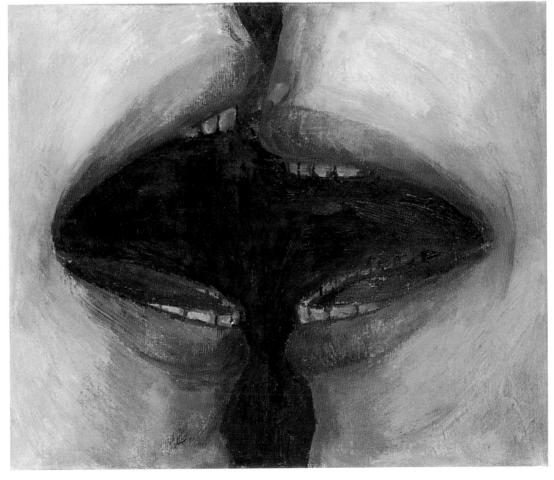

RECURRENT DREAM NO. 2

The landscape in my recurrent dream is unlike any I have seen, where the land meets the sea.
A road travels up and around hills, an animated ribbon between heaving contours,
where trees and houses cling on to land in roaring winds that whip the sea into great pyramids
of silver foaming spray.

Everything is pitch dark, just the sensation of intense movement,
and brilliant shafts of water coloured light from an unknown source.
In the dream I always feel a sense of great exhilaration, of being part of a dramatic occurrence,
a wonderful re-enactment of a previous treasured experience.

I know I have been here before.

Thanks

To my father for taking me to the National Gallery when I was 12
To Michael Fussell for his unquestioning help with my work
To Anthony Perry for all his support and making this book a reality
And to Bruce Bernard, Derek Birdsall and John McEwen

And to all my family, friends, collectors, and the keepers, curators,
and gallery owners who went out of their way to show my work.

EW